187216

PowerKids Readers:

# The Bilingual Library of the United States of America™

# FLORIDA

### JOSÉ MARÍA OBREGÓN

Traducción al español: María Cristina Brusca

The Rosen Publishing Group's
PowerKids Press™ & Editorial Buenas Letras™
New York

Published in 2005 by The Rosen Publishing Group, Inc.
29 East 21st Street, New York, NY 10010

First Edition

Photo Credits: Cover, p. 30 (Palm Tree) © Rick Bostick/Index Stock Imagery Inc.;
p. 5 © Joseph Sohm; Visions of America/Corbis; p. 9 © Patrick Ward/Corbis; p. 11 © Jeff
Greenberg/Index Stock Imagery Inc.; p. 13 © North Wind Picture Archives; p. 15 © Richard
Cummins/Corbis; p. 19 © John Anderson/Index Stock Imagery Inc.; p. 21 © Nik
Wheeler/Corbis; p. 23 © Kevin Fleming/Corbis; pp. 25, 30 (Capitol) © Reuters/Corbis;
p. 30 (Orange Blossom) © Charles Marden Fitch/SuperStock; p. 30 (Moonstone) © Omni
Photo Communications Inc./Index Stock Imagery Inc.; p. 31 (Osceola) © Bettman/Corbis;
p. 31 (Hurston) © Corbis; p. 31 (Reno) © Wally McNamee/Corbis; p. 31 (Bujones) © Clive
Barda/PAL/Topham/The Image Works; p. 31 (Evert) © Maiman Rick/Corbis Sygma;
p. 31 (Estefan) © Mitchell Gerber/Corbis; p. 31 (Fort) © Kent Dufault/Index Stock Imagery
Inc.; p. 31 (Swamp) © Catherine Wessel/Corbis.

**Library of Congress Cataloging-in-Publication Data**

Obregón, José María, 1963–
Florida / José María Obregón; Traducción al español: María Cristina Brusca.— 1st ed.
    p. ; cm. — (The bilingual library of the United States of America)
Includes text in English and Spanish.
Includes bibliographical references and index.
ISBN 1-4042-3074-2 (lib. bdg.)
1. Florida—Juvenile literature. I. Brusca, María Cristina. II. Title. III. Series.
F311.3.O27 2006
975.9-dc22

2004028767

Manufactured in the United States of America

Due to the changing nature of Internet links, Editorial Buenas
Letras has developed an online list of Web sites related to the
subject of this book. This site is updated regularly. Please use
this link to access the list:

http://www.buenasletraslinks.com/ls/florida

# Contents

# Contenido

## Welcome to Florida

These are the flag and the seal of the state of Florida. You can see a Seminole woman on the seal. The Seminole have lived in Florida for more than 500 years!

---

## Bienvenidos a Florida

Estos son la bandera y el escudo de Florida. En el escudo puedes ver a una mujer semínola. ¡Los semínolas han vivido en Florida por más de 500 años!

The Florida Flag and State Seal

La bandera y el escudo de Florida

## Florida Geography

Florida borders the states of Georgia and Alabama. Florida is a peninsula. It is connected to the land on only one side. The rest of the state is surrounded by water.

---

## Geografía de Florida

Florida limita con los estados de Georgia y Alabama. Florida es una península, conectada al territorio por uno de sus lados. El resto del estado está rodeado de agua.

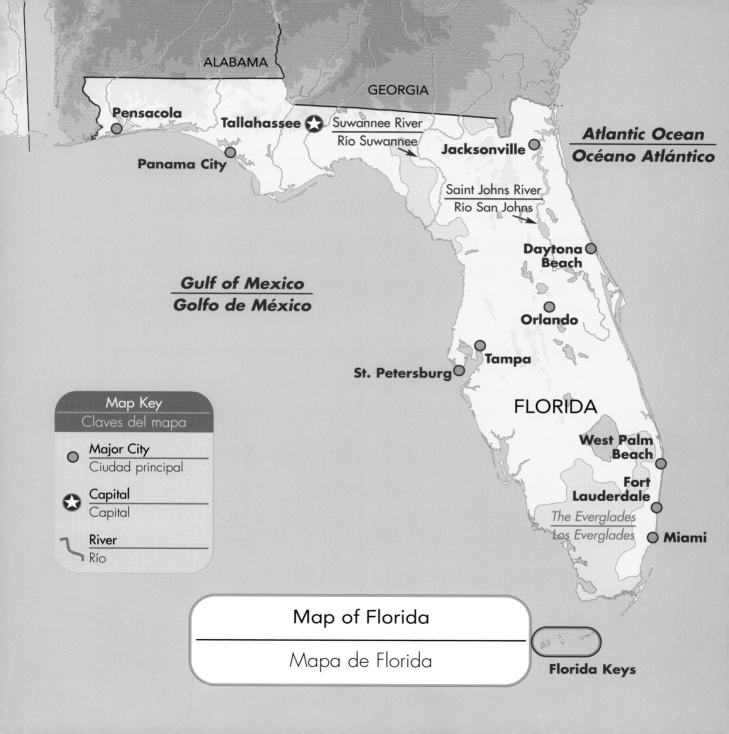

ALABAMA

GEORGIA

Pensacola

Tallahassee ★ Suwannee River
Río Suwannee

Panama City

Jacksonville

**Atlantic Ocean**
**Océano Atlántico**

Saint Johns River
Río San Johns

Daytona
Beach

*Gulf of Mexico*
*Golfo de México*

Orlando

Tampa

St. Petersburg

FLORIDA

West Palm
Beach

Fort
Lauderdale

*The Everglades*
*Los Everglades*

Miami

## Map Key
Claves del mapa

⬤ Major City
Ciudad principal

★ Capital
Capital

River
Río

## Map of Florida

Mapa de Florida

**Florida Keys**

Florida has four national parks. The Everglades National Park is the largest swamp in the state. A swamp is an area of land flooded with water.

---

Florida tiene cuatro parques nacionales. El Parque Nacional Everglades es el pantano más grande del estado. Un pantano es una porción de tierra inundada de agua.

An Alligator at the Everglades National Park

Un caimán en el Parque Nacional Everglades

Most of America's oranges are grown in Florida. Florida also produces juice from grapefruits, limes, and lemons. Orange juice was named the state drink of Florida in 1967.

---

La mayoría de las naranjas de Norteamérica se producen en Florida. Florida también produce jugo de pomelo o toronja, lima y limón. El jugo de naranja fue nombrado la bebida del estado de Florida en el año 1967.

Oranges Are Important for Florida's Economy

Las naranjas son importantes para la economía de Florida

## Florida History

Juan Ponce de León was the first European to arrive in Florida in 1513. He named the area La Florida, which is Spanish for "land of flowers."

---

## Historia de Florida

Juan Ponce de León fue el primer europeo en llegar a Florida en 1513. Ponce de León llamó a esta región La Florida, que quiere decir "tierra de las flores".

Juan Ponce de León

The Spanish explorers set up a fort in the city of St. Augustine in 1565. This city became the first European settlement in America.

---

En 1565, los exploradores españoles establecieron la ciudad y el fuerte de San Agustín. Esta ciudad fue el primer poblado europeo en Norteamérica.

NO FISHING
THIS AREA

The Bridge of Lions in St. Augustine

El Puente de los Leones en San Agustín

Andrew Jackson was the first governor of the Florida Territory. In 1829, Jackson became the seventh president of the United States of America.

---

Andrew Jackson fue el primer gobernador del Territorio de Florida. En 1829, Jackson fue nombrado el séptimo presidente de los Estados Unidos de América.

Andrew Jackson on a Twenty-dollar Bill

Andrew Jackson en un billete de veinte dólares

## Living in Florida

The weather in Florida is warm and sunny. The good weather brings people from all over the world. Only three states have more people than Florida.

---

## La vida en Florida

El clima en Florida es cálido y soleado. El buen clima atrae a la gente de todo el mundo. Solamente tres estados tienen más habitantes que Florida.

**People Enjoy the Beaches in Florida**

Gente disfrutando las playas de Florida

Many Hispanics live in Florida. People from the island of Cuba and other countries in Latin America celebrate their holidays in Florida.

---

Muchos hispanos viven en Florida. Gente de la isla de Cuba y de otros países de América Latina celebran sus fiestas en Florida.

Carnival in Calle Ocho in Miami, Florida

Carnaval en la Calle Ocho en Miami, Florida

## Florida Today

More than 40 million people visit the theme parks and the beaches of Florida every year. Visitors are very important for Florida's business.

---

## Florida, hoy

Cada año, más de 40 millones de personas visitan los parques de diversiones y las playas de Florida. Los turistas son muy importantes para los negocios de Florida.

Typhoon Lagoon in Orlando, Florida
_____
Typhoon Lagoon en Orlando, Florida

Jacksonville, Miami, Tampa, St. Petersburg, Orlando, and Fort Lauderdale are important cities in Florida. Tallahassee is the capital of the state.

---

Jacksonville, Miami, Tampa, St. Petersburg, Orlando y Fort Lauderdale son ciudades importantes de Florida. Tallahassee es la capital del estado.

The New and Old Capitol Buildings in Tallahassee

El antiguo y el nuevo capitolio en Tallahassee

# Activity:
## Let's Draw the Map of Florida

# Actividad:
## Dibujemos el mapa de Florida

**1**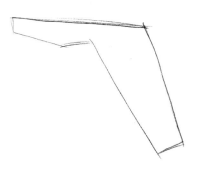

Draw the angled shape as shown.

Dibuja una forma angulosa siguiendo el ejemplo

**2**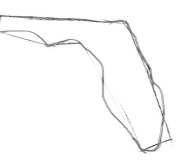

Add curves to the angled shape.

Agrega curvas a la forma angulosa

**3**

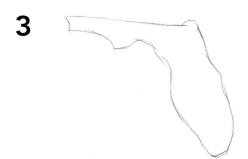

Erase extra lines. You just drew the outline of the state of Florida.

Borra las líneas innecesarias. Ya has dibujado el contorno del estado de Florida.

**4**

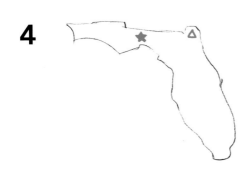

Draw a five-pointed star for Tallahassee, the state capital. Draw a triangle in the upper right for St. Augustine.

Dibuja una estrella de cinco puntas para la capital del estado: Tallahassee. Traza un triángulo, arriba a la derecha, para San Agustín.

**5**

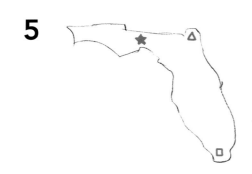

Draw a square at the bottom for the Everglades.

Dibuja un cuadrado, abajo, para indicar los Everglades.

# Timeline

# Cronología

| Timeline | | Cronología |
|---|---|---|
| Spanish explorer Juan Ponce de León arrives in Florida. | **1513** | El explorador español Juan Ponce de León llega a la Florida. |
| Spanish colonists establish St. Augustine. | **1565** | Los colonos españoles establecen San Agustín. |
| Florida becomes the Twenty-seventh state in the United States. | **1845** | Florida se convierte en el estado número veintisiete de los Estados Unidos. |
| The first missile launch takes place in Cape Canaveral. | **1950** | El primer lanzamiento de un misil se realiza en Cabo Cañaveral. |
| More than 20,000 Cubans leave Cuba and settle in Florida. | **1959** | Más de 20,000 cubanos dejan Cuba y se establecen en Florida. |
| Hurricane Andrew strikes southern Florida. | **1992** | El Huracán Andrew golpea el sur de Florida. |
| The U.S. presidential election is decided by Florida's electoral votes. | **2000** | La elección presidencial de E.U.A. es decidida por los votos electorales de Florida. |

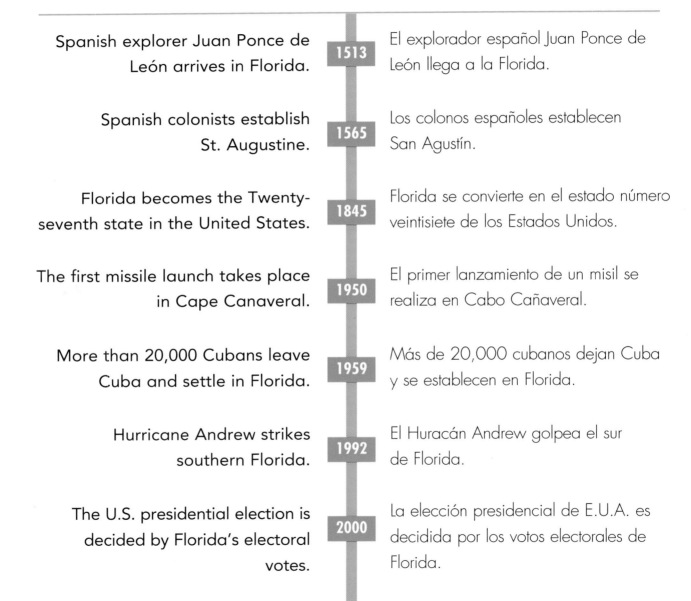

| Florida Events | Eventos en Florida |
|---|---|
| **January–March**<br>Old Island Days in Key West | Enero–Marzo<br>Días de la isla vieja, en Key West |
| **February**<br>Florida Citrus Festival<br>in Winter Haven<br>Florida State Fair in Tampa | Febrero<br>Festival de los cítricos, en Winter Haven<br>Feria del estado de Florida, en Tampa |
| **March**<br>Motorcycle Week in Daytona Beach | Marzo<br>Semana de la motocicleta, en Daytona Beach |
| **April**<br>Easter Week Festival in St. Augustine | Abril<br>Festival de la semana de Pascua,<br>en San Agustín |
| **May**<br>Fiesta of Five Flags in Pensacola | Mayo<br>Fiesta de las cinco banderas, en Pensacola |
| **June**<br>Pensacola Shark Rodeo in Pensacola | Junio<br>Rodeo del tiburón, en Pensacola |
| **August**<br>Days in Spain in St. Augustine | Agosto<br>Días en España, en San Agustín |
| **November**<br>Beaux Arts Promenade in the Park<br>in Fort Lauderdale | Noviembre<br>Paseo de las Bellas Artes, en Fort<br>Lauderdale |
| **December**<br>Gator Bowl Festival and Football<br>Game in Jacksonville<br>Florida Citrus Bowl Football Game<br>in Orlando | Diciembre<br>Festival Gator Bowl y Juego de Fútbol, en<br>Jacksonville<br>Juego de Fútbol Florida Citrus Bowl, en<br>Orlando |

# Florida Facts/Datos sobre Florida

<u>Population</u>
16 million

<u>Población</u>
16 millones

<u>Capital</u>
Tallahassee

<u>Capital</u>
Tallahassee

<u>State Motto</u>
"In God We Trust"

<u>Lema del estado</u>
En Dios confiamos

<u>State Flower</u>
Orange Blossom

<u>Flor del estado</u>
Azahar

<u>State Bird</u>
Mockingbird

<u>Ave del estado</u>
Sinsonte

<u>State Nickname</u>
"The Sunshine State"

<u>Mote del estado</u>
El estado del sol

<u>State Tree</u>
Sabal Palm

<u>Árbol del estado</u>
Palmera Sabal

<u>State Song</u>
"The Swanee River"

<u>Canción del estado</u>
"El Río Swanee"

<u>State Gemstone</u>
Moonstone

<u>Piedra preciosa</u>
Piedra de luna

# Famous Floridians/Floridianos famosos

**Osceola**
*(1804?–1838)*
Seminole Leader
Líder seminola

**Zora Neale Hurston**
*(1891–1960)*
Author
Autor

**Janet Reno**
*(1938–   )*
Politician
Política

**Fernando Bujones**
*(1955–   )*
Dancer
Bailarín

**Chris Evert**
*(1954–   )*
Tennis Player
Jugadora de tenis

**Gloria Estefan**
*(1957–   )*
Singer
Cantante

## Words to Know/Palabras que debes saber

**border**
frontera

**fort**
fuerte

**peninsula**
península

**swamp**
pantano

# Here are more books to read about Florida:
## Otros libros que puedes leer sobre la Florida:

**In English/En inglés:**

*Florida*
By Barbara A. Somervill
Children's Press, 2001

**In Spanish/En español:**

*Florida, el estado del sol*
by Chui, Patricia
Traducción al español: Carlos Porras
World Almanac Library, 2003

Words in English: 256

Palabras en español: 274

# Index

# Índice

What a perfect dog!

Clifford had made some new friends.
What a perfect class trip!

The other whales swam to her side.

The little whale seemed to know
that she was home.
She splashed the water with her flipper.

In no time at all, we were far out in the bay.

A boat was waiting. We all got on board.

He ran through the busy traffic to the dock.

Clifford picked her up.

The whale trainer got the baby whale to
swim onto a canvas sling.

It was time to return the baby whale to the ocean.

But the truck had broken down.

I had an idea.

In another tank there was a baby whale. She had been rescued from some fishing nets.

Clifford was very thankful!

A friendly porpoise came to help.

That was not a good idea.

Then he got curious about the pool next to the seals.
He moved closer to get a better look.

DO NOT PUT HANDS IN POOL !

Clifford got it for her.

One seal tossed the ball a little too far.

We saw some seals in an outdoor pool.
They were playing with a beach ball.

The class went on to our next stop — the aquarium.

Clifford felt bad. He tried to put the skeleton back together again.
He did a pretty good job.

Clifford got excited when he saw the dinosaur skeleton.
He *loves* bones. Uh-oh ...

187217

PowerKids Readers:

# The Bilingual Library of the United States of America™

Bilingual Edition
English/Spanish
Edición bilingüe

# GEORGIA

**VANESSA BROWN**

TRADUCCIÓN AL ESPAÑOL: MARÍA CRISTINA BRUSCA

The Rosen Publishing Group's
PowerKids Press™ & **Editorial Buenas Letras**™
New York

Published in 2005 by The Rosen Publishing Group, Inc.
29 East 21st Street, New York, NY 10010

First Edition

Photo Credits: Cover © 1997 Digital Vision; p. 7 © 2002 Geoatlas; pp. 9, 31 (Mountain Chain) © Jerry Cooke, Inc./Animals Animals/Earth Scenes; pp. 11, 23, 31 (Business) © Kevin Fleming/Corbis; pp. 13, 17, 31 (Carter, King) © Bettmann/Corbis; pp. 15, 31 (Charles, Civil War) © Corbis; p. 19 © Free Agents Limited/Corbis; p. 21 Courtesy of Colquitt Miller Arts Council; pp. 25, 30 (Capital) © Joseph Sohm; ChromoSohm Inc./Corbis; pp. 26, 30 (State Nickname, The Peach State) © Bob Krist/Corbis; p. 30 (Cherokee Rose) © John Pontier/Earth Scenes; p. 30 (Brown Thrasher) © Ron Austing; Frank Lane Picture Agency/ Corbis; p. 30 (Live Oak) © Raymond Gehman/Corbis; p. 30 (Quartz) © José Manuel Sanchis Calvete/Corbis; p. 31 (Cobb) © Getty Images; p. 31 (Mitchell) © AFP/Getty Images; p. 31 (Walker) © Roger Ressmeyer/Corbis

Library of Congress Cataloging-in-Publication Data

Brown, Vanessa, 1963–
Georgia / Vanessa Brown ; traducción al español, María Cristina Brusca.— 1st ed.
p. cm. — (The bilingual library of the United States of America) Includes bibliographical references and index. ISBN 1-4042-3075-0 (library binding)
1. Georgia–Juvenile literature. I. Title. II. Series.

F286.3.B76 2005
975.8'04—dc22

2005001247

Manufactured in the United States of America

Due to the changing nature of Internet links, Editorial Buenas Letras has developed an online list of Web sites related to the subject of this book. This site is updated regularly. Please use this link to access the list:

http://www.buenasletraslinks.com/ls/georgia

# Contents

# Contenido

# Welcome to Georgia

These are the flag and the seal of the state of Georgia. The flag was adopted on May 2003. The 13 stars around the seal remind us that Georgia was one of the original 13 colonies.

---

# Bienvenidos a Georgia

Estos son la bandera y el escudo de Georgia. La bandera fue adoptada en mayo del 2003. Las 13 estrellas que rodean el escudo nos recuerdan que Georgia fue una de las 13 colonias.

## Georgia Flag and State Seal

Bandera y escudo de Georgia

## Georgia Geography

Georgia borders South Carolina, North Carolina, Tennessee, Alabama, and Florida. Georgia's eastern coast borders the Atlantic Ocean.

---

## Geografía de Georgia

Georgia linda con Carolina del Sur, Carolina del Norte, Tennessee, Alabama y Florida. La costa este de Georgia bordea el océano Atlántico.

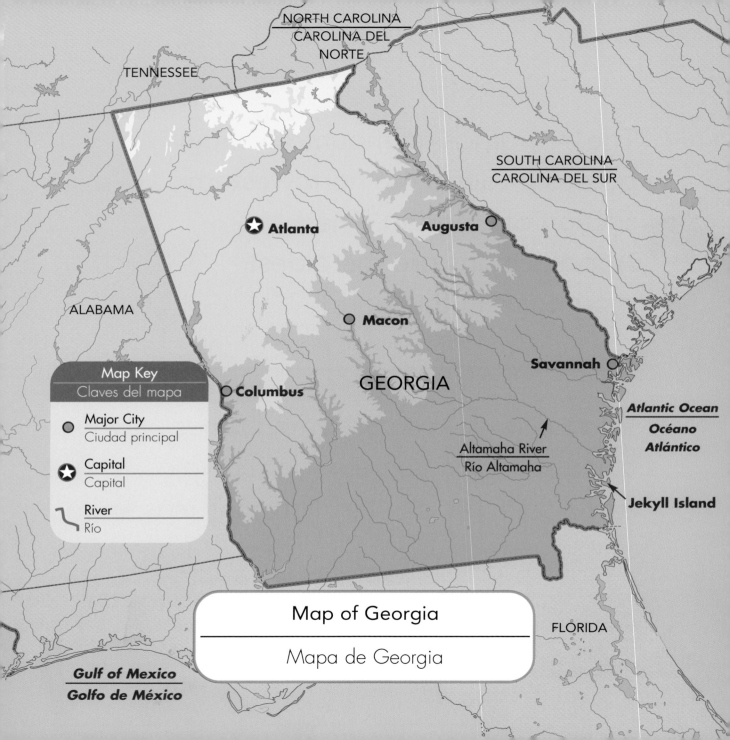

NORTH CAROLINA
CAROLINA DEL NORTE

TENNESSEE

SOUTH CAROLINA
CAROLINA DEL SUR

ALABAMA

★ Atlanta

○ Augusta

○ Macon

○ Savannah

**GEORGIA**

○ Columbus

Atlantic Ocean
Océano Atlántico

Altamaha River
Río Altamaha

Jekyll Island

| Map Key |
|---|
| Claves del mapa |
| ● Major City / Ciudad principal |
| ★ Capital / Capital |
| ∿ River / Río |

FLORIDA

Map of Georgia

Mapa de Georgia

Gulf of Mexico
Golfo de México

The Appalachian mountain chain passes through the northwestern section of Georgia. The Appalachians are the oldest mountains in the world!

---

La cadena de montañas Apalaches cruza la región noroeste de Georgia. ¡Los Apalaches son las montañas más antiguas del mundo!

Appalachian National Scenic Trail

Ruta Panorámica Nacional Apalaches

## Georgia History

Three Native American nations lived in Georgia in the 1500s. They were the Cherokee, the Creek, and the Seminole.

---

## Historia de Georgia

En los años 1500, tres tribus de nativos americanos vivían en Georgia. Éstas eran las tribus Cherokee, Creek y Seminola.

Cherokee Dancers in the Chehaw National Indian Festival

Danzantes cherokees en el Festival Nacional Indio Chehaw

A British man named James E. Oglethorpe founded the colony of Georgia in 1733. He named the colony after George II, king of England.

_____

Un británico, llamado James E. Oglethorpe, fundó la colonia de Georgia en 1733. Oglethorpe nombró la colonia en honor al rey George II de Inglaterra.

James E. Oglethorpe, Founder of Georgia

James E. Oglethorpe, fundador de Georgia

Georgia took part in the Civil War. The Civil War was fought between the North and the South from 1861 to 1865. The Battle of Chickamauga was fought in northwest Georgia. It was an important victory for the South.

---

Georgia participó en la Guerra Civil. La Guerra Civil se desarrollo entre el Norte y el Sur, de 1861 a 1865. La Batalla de Chickamauga se peleo en el noroeste de Georgia. Esta fue una importante victoria para el Sur.

Battle of Chickamauga in the Summer of 1863

Batalla de Chickamauga, en el verano de 1863

Dr. Martin Luther King Jr. was born in Atlanta in 1929. He led the civil rights movement in the 1960s. This movement gave African Americans the right to work and education.

---

El Dr. Martin Luther King Jr. nació en Atlanta en 1929. El Dr. King lideró el movimiento por los derechos civiles en los años 1960. Este movimiento le dio a los afroamericanos el derecho al trabajo y a la educación.

Martin Luther King Jr. in 1963
_____

Martin Luther King Jr. en 1963

## Living in Georgia

More than half of Georgia's population lives around the city of Atlanta. Atlanta is the capital of the state.

---

## La vida en Georgia

Más de la mitad de la población de Georgia vive en los alrededores de la ciudad de Atlanta. Atlanta es la capital del estado.

Atlanta is the Capital of Georgia

Atlanta es la captial de Georgia

Georgians are proud of their history. *The Swamp Gravy: Georgia's Official Folk Life Play* is a show that tells real stories of people in Georgia. *The Swamp Gravy* is performed every year.

---

Los georgianos están orgullosos de su historia. La obra de teatro folclórico oficial de Georgia es *The Swamp Gravy*. Ésta es una obra de teatro que cuenta historias de la vida real de los pobladores de Georgia y se presenta todos los años.

A Scene from *The Swamp Gravy*

Una escena de la obra *The Swamp Gravy*

## Georgia Today

Georgia is an important business center. Many big companies such as CNN and Coca-Cola are based in Georgia. Georgia is known as the Empire State of the South.

---

## Georgia, hoy

Georgia es un importante centro de negocios. Muchas compañías como CNN y Coca-Cola tienen sus oficinas centrales en Georgia. Georgia es conocido como el Estado Imperial del Sur.

Coca-Cola Offices in Atlanta
———————————————
Oficinas de la Coca-Cola en Atlanta

Atlanta, Savannah, and Columbus are important cities in Georgia. Atlanta is the capital of Georgia.

---

Atlanta, Savannah y Columbus son ciudades importantes de Georgia. Atlanta es la capital de Georgia.

State Capitol in Atlanta, Georgia

Capitolio del estado en Atlanta, Georgia

# Activity:
## Let's Draw the Georgia Peach
Georgia is also known as the Peach State

---

# Actividad:
## Dibujemos el durazno de Georgia
Georgia es también conocido como el Estado-Durazno

**1**

Start by drawing a box.

Comienza por dibujar una caja.

**2**

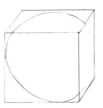

Draw a round shape inside the box.

Dibuja una forma redonda adentro de la caja.

**3**

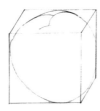

Draw three curved lines at the top of the circle.

Dibuja tres líneas curvas en la parte de arriba del círculo.

**4**

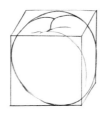

Draw more curved lines from the top of the circle, as shown here.

Dibuja más líneas curvas desde la parte de arriba del círculo, como ves en el ejemplo.

**5**

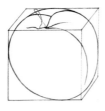

Make a stem by drawing a thin teardrop shape at the top of the peach.

Traza el tallo, en forma de lágrima delgada, sobre la parte de arriba del durazno.

**6**

Add shading to your peach and erase extra lines.

Borra las líneas innecesarias y sombrea tu durazno.

# Timeline

# Cronología

| | | |
|---|---|---|
| Hernándo de Soto leads the first exploration to Georgia. | **1540** | Hernando de Soto dirige la primera expedición a Georgia. |
| James E. Oglethorpe establishes Savannah. | **1733** | James E.Oglethorpe funda Savannah. |
| Eli Whitney invents the cotton gin. | **1783** | Eli Whitney inventa la desmotadora de algodon. |
| Georgia joins the Confederate States of America. | **1861** | Georgia se une a la Confederación de Estados de América. |
| The first African American is elected mayor of Atlanta. | **1973** | Es elegido el primer alcalde afroamericano de Atlanta. |
| Atlanta hosts the Summer Olympics. | **1996** | Atlanta es la sede de las Olimpíadas. |
| Georgia adopts a new state flag. | **2003** | Georgia adopta una nueva bandera del estado. |

# Georgia Events

|  |  |
|---:|:---|
| **January** | |
| German Carnival in Helen | |
| **February** | |
| Georgia Day in Savannah | |
| **March** | |
| Statewide Tours of Historical Homes | |
| **April** | |
| Masters Tournament at Augusta National Golf Course | |
| National Arts Festival in Atlanta | |
| **May** | |
| Andersonville Historic Fair | |
| **July** | |
| Georgia Shakespeare Festival in Atlanta | |
| **October** | |
| Georgia National Fair in Perry | |
| **December** | |
| Christmas on Jekyll Island | |

# Eventos en Georgia

**Enero**
Carnaval alemán, en Helen

**Febrero**
Día de Georgia, en Savannah

**Marzo**
Gira de visitas a las casas históricas, en todo el estado

**Abril**
Torneo de maestros en el Campo Nacional de Golf de Augusta
Festival de las Artes de Atlanta

**Mayo**
Feria histórica de Andersonville

**Julio**
Festival Shakespeare, en Atlanta

**Octubre**
Feria Nacional de Georgia, en Perry

**Diciembre**
Navidad en Isla Jekyll

# Georgia Facts/Datos sobre Georgia

<u>Population</u>
8 million

<u>Población</u>
8 millones

<u>Capital</u>
Atlanta

<u>Capital</u>
Atlanta

<u>State Motto</u>
Wisdom, Justice and
Moderation

<u>Lema del estado</u>
Sabiduría, justicia y
moderación

<u>State Flower</u>
Cherokee rose

<u>Flor del estado</u>
Rosa Cherokee

<u>State Bird</u>
Brown thrasher

<u>Ave del estado</u>
Sinsonte castaño

<u>State Nickname</u>
Empire State of the South,
The Peach State

<u>Mote del estado</u>
Estado Imperial del
Sur, Estado-Durazno

<u>State Tree</u>
Live oak

<u>Árbol del estado</u>
Roble

<u>State Song</u>
"Georgia on My Mind"

<u>Canción del estado</u>
"Georgia en mi
pensamiento"

<u>State Gemstone</u>
Quartz

<u>Piedra preciosa</u>
Cuarzo

# Famous Georgians/Georgianos famosos

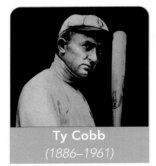

**Ty Cobb**
*(1886–1961)*

Baseball player
Jugador de béisbol

**Margaret Mitchell**
*(1900–1949)*

Author
Escritora

**Jimmy Carter**
*(1924—    )*

U.S. President
Presidente de E.U.A.

**Dr. Martin Luther King Jr.** *(1929–1968)*

Civil rights leader
Líder de los derechos civiles

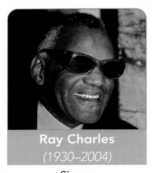

**Ray Charles**
*(1930–2004)*

Singer
Cantante

**Alice Walker**
*(1944—    )*

Poet
Poeta

# Words to Know/Palabras que debes saber

**border**
frontera

**business**
negocios

**Civil War**
Guerra Civil

**mountain chain**
cadena de montañas

# Here are more books to read about Georgia:
## Otros libros que puedes leer sobre Georgia:

**In English/En inglés:**

*Georgia*
From Sea to Shining Sea
By: Stechschulte, Pattie
Children's Press, 2001

*How to Draw Georgia's Sights and Symbols*
A Kids Guide to Drawing America
By: Quasha, Jennifer
PowerKids Press, 2002

Words in English: 276

Palabras en español: 316

# Index

# Índice